WITHDRAWN

D1737858

Learning Resources Center
University of Wyoming Libraries
Laramie, WY 82070

SEEDS TO PLANTS

Learning Resources Center
University of Wyoming Libraries
Laramie, WY 82070

© Aladdin Books Ltd 1990

Design	David West
	Children's Book Design
Editorial Planning	Clark Robinson Limited
Picture researcher	Emma Krikler
Illustrator	Neil Bullpit
Consultant	Andy Byfield
	Botanist active in conservation and research

First published in
the United States in 1991 by
Gloucester Press
387 Park Avenue South
New York NY 10016

Printed in Belgium

All rights reserved

Library of Congress Cataloging-in-Publication Data

Bates, Jeffrey.
    Seeds to plants : projects with biology / Jeffrey Bates.
    p. cm. -- (Hands on science)
    Includes index.
    Summary: Explores the biology of seeds and how they develop into
plants.
    ISBN 0-531-17292-9
    1. Plants--Juvenile literature. 2. Seeds--Juvenile literature. 3.
Plants--Development--Juvenile literature. [1. Plants--Development. 2.
Seeds. 3. Experiments.] I. Title. II. Series.
QK49.B33 1991
582--dc20   90-45659   CIP   AC

582
Bat

HANDS · ON · SCIENCE

SEEDS TO PLANTS

Dr Jeffrey Bates

GLOUCESTER PRESS
New York · London · Toronto · Sydney

CONTENTS

This book is about plants and how they grow and develop — from seeds to fully grown flowering plants. The book tells you about the different parts of plants. It also describes the function that each part has in the life cycle of plants. There are "hands on" projects for you to try, which use everyday items as equipment, and involve common plants.

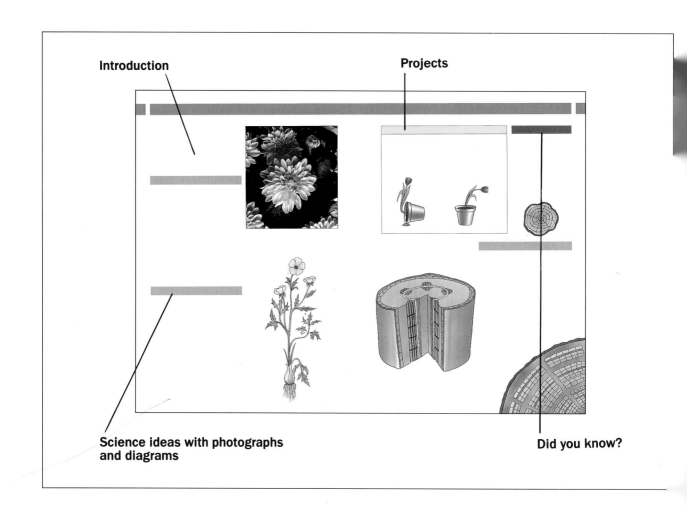

Introduction

Projects

Science ideas with photographs and diagrams

Did you know?

INTRODUCTION

Plants grow all around us and we often pay little attention to them. But without plants, our lives and the lives of all other animals would be impossible. Plants produce the oxygen we breathe. They also trap the energy in sunlight, which is the original source of energy in all of our food.

People have studied plants since long before the start of written history because they depend on them for food, and also for fuel, clothing, building materials and medicines. The scientific study of plants is known as botany. The earliest botanists spent much of their time discovering and naming the different types or species of plant. They also looked for plants that would help to cure diseases.

Today, botanists use the latest scientific techniques to study how plants work. The knowledge that botanists gain is used in many ways to benefit us. Examples of these benefits are the breeding of better varieties of crops, and the use of chemicals in plants as medicines.

Plants make food and oxygen by using solar energy.

Plants cannot move around like animals. This is because they need a supply of water and mineral salts from the soil. They get these through their roots. Seeds form on parent plants after flowering. Each seed contains a young plant called an embryo. Seeds allow plants to spread to new places and to survive dry seasons.

STRUCTURE

A tough coat, the testa, surrounds the seed and protects the embryo. There is a small hole in the testa called the micropyle. Inside the seed are leaflike structures called cotyledons. Flowering plants are divided into two groups, depending on how many cotyledons they have. Lilies, grasses and palms are known as the monocotyledons and have one per seed. Herbs, shrubs and broad-leaf trees, the dicotyledons, have two.

The embryo has a root known as the radicle and a tiny shoot called the plumule. Most seeds contain a food store for the embryo. Seeds form inside fruits. Fruits give the seed extra protection and help to disperse the seeds.

△ Nuts are very hard fruits.

▽ Lupin pods are explosive fruits. The pericarp (shell) suddenly splits and twists when it dries, throwing the seeds out.

Pericarp

Seed

EXPLOSIVE FRUIT

Remains of petals and stamens

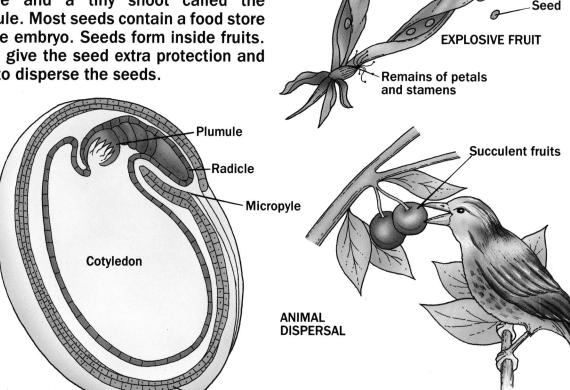

Plumule

Radicle

Micropyle

Cotyledon

Testa

Succulent fruits

ANIMAL DISPERSAL

△ Peas and beans contain food in large cotyledons. These seeds are valuable food for humans.

△ Succulent fruits have stony seeds. These pass through animals that eat them and are deposited with feces.

DISPERSAL

It is important that young plants start life a good distance from their parents, so that they can get plenty of light and nutrients. The way in which seeds are carried away from the parent plant is called dispersal. Seed dispersal usually involves natural forces, because plants cannot move themselves.

Fruits are important in the dispersal of seeds. In botany, the name "fruit" includes many structures besides the familiar fruits that we enjoy eating. Fruits develop from a part of the flower called the ovary. This surrounds the seed. The wall of the ovary (the pericarp) forms the outside of the fruit.

Fruits that open to release or throw out seeds are known as dehiscent fruits. Forces develop in the pericarp as it dries and cause it to split. Some dehiscent fruits produce very small seeds, which are easily blown away. Fruits that do not open are known as indehiscent fruits. These rely only on either wind, animals or water for dispersal.

△▷ Each part of a dandelion "clock" breaks off to be carried by the wind. In the lime, a leaflike wing breaks off with the fruit and works just like the sycamore fruit.

Dried bract on stalk

Lime fruit

Ovary

WIND DISPERSAL

▷ Sycamore fruits have wings that make them spin and fall slowly. This allows them to be blown quite long distances by the wind.

Sycamore

Ovary

Wing extensions of ovary

DID YOU KNOW?

Seeds of the coconut palm are dispersed by the sea. The large woody coconuts are covered by a fibrous husk and can float for a long time. Ocean currents sometimes carry them for great distances.

Hooked fruits on cat's tail

ANIMAL DISPERSAL

◁ Many fruits have hooks or spines. These catch in the fur of animals, and in this way the seed is carried away.

Learning Resources Center
University of Wyoming Libraries

If a seed is dispersed to a suitable place, the embryo inside eventually starts to grow. The first stage of growth is called germination. Before it can germinate, the seed absorbs water from the soil. It also needs oxygen and the right temperature. The embryo grows into a seedling using food stored in the seed.

DORMANCY

Many ripe seeds will not germinate at first, even if they are placed in good conditions. These are called dormant seeds. Seeds become dormant so as not to grow at times when conditions would normally be too poor for the seedlings to survive. Dormant seeds start to grow only after they receive a signal. In some seeds, the signal is a period of cold followed by warmer temperatures. This tells the seed that winter has passed.

△ Most seeds dry out as they ripen, for example, the seeds in these poppy pods.

ABSORBING WATER

Put equal layers of dried peas or beans into two jars. Cover the seeds in one of the jars with a layer of water.

Do not add any water to the control jar. This one is set up to show what the seeds were like at the start.

After one day, the seed layer in the first jar is deeper. The seeds have absorbed water and swollen.

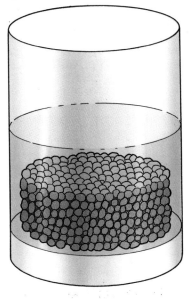

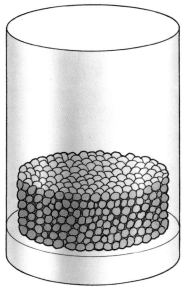

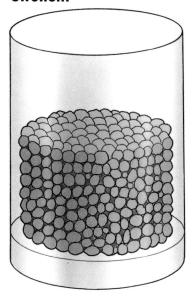

Start of experiment

Control

After one day

RAPID GROWTH

Once a seed germinates, rapid changes start to happen. First, the radicle swells and pushes its way through the testa. It then grows down into the soil and absorbs water and minerals for the seedling. Food stored in the seed is turned into forms that can be used by the seedling as it grows. The plumule grows upward to form the shoot. When the shoot reaches the light, it turns green and starts to make its own food using sunlight. Making food using energy from light is known as photosynthesis.

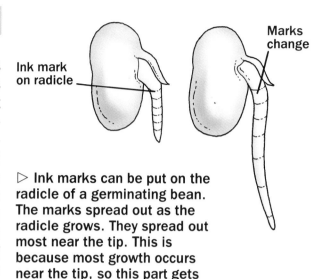

Ink mark on radicle

Marks change

▷ Ink marks can be put on the radicle of a germinating bean. The marks spread out as the radicle grows. They spread out most near the tip. This is because most growth occurs near the tip, so this part gets longer more quickly.

WATER IN GERMINATION

Set up four jars as shown in the pictures. Use peas sold for use as seed. Cover each jar with plastic wrap. See which peas germinate. Peas will germinate if they are kept moist. But when covered with water, they get too little oxygen.

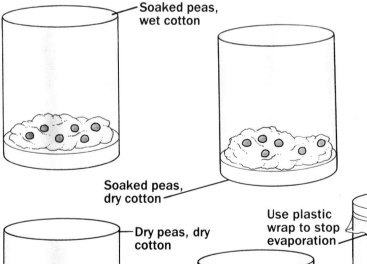

Soaked peas, wet cotton

Soaked peas, dry cotton

Dry peas, dry cotton

Use plastic wrap to stop evaporation

Soaked peas covered with water

DID YOU KNOW?

Many dormant seeds can remain alive for more than 10 years. In nature, a "seed bank," composed of dormant seeds, often builds up in the soil. If all of the parent plants are killed — for example, by a fire — there is a good chance they will be replaced from the seed bank. Scientists store rare or important seeds in refrigerators. Cold can slow down the rate at which dormant seeds die.

LEARNING RESOURCES CENTER
UNIVERSITY OF WYOMING LIBRARIES
LARAMIE, WY 82071

PEAS

The way in which seeds germinate depends on the number of cotyledons and what their function is.

The garden pea is a dicotyledon. In pea seeds, the main function of the cotyledons is to store food. After the radicle has pushed its way out of the seed, the shoot begins to grow. For a short time, growth happens only in the part of the shoot between the cotyledons and the plumule. This part is called the epicotyl. The plumule is a delicate region at the tip of the shoot. Later it will be the main area where shoot growth occurs. The shoot is bent over as it is pushed through the soil. This protects the plumule from damage. Once it has emerged from the soil, the shoot straightens and the first leaves form. The cotyledons remain inside the seed and never emerge above ground. When their food store has been used, they shrivel up.

This type of germination, where the cotyledons never function as true leaves, is called hypogeal germination. The broad bean, acorn and hazelnut also have hypogeal germination.

▽ Germination starts with the appearance of the radicle (A). As it grows, it produces fine root hairs which help it to absorb water and salts (B).

▷ The bent shoot protects the plumule as it emerges from the soil (C). The plumule forms leaves and shoots. New roots grow from the radicle (D,E).

A   B   C   D   E

SUNFLOWERS

The sunflower is a dicotyledon, like the garden pea. Each sunflower "seed" is actually an indehiscent fruit that contains one seed.

Germination starts in the sunflower in the same way as in the pea. The radicle bursts out of the seed coat and fruit, then grows downward. Next, however, the length of stem between the radicle and the cotyledons starts to elongate. This part of the stem is called the hypocotyl. By lengthening, it pulls the cotyledons up into the air. Again, the stem is bent to protect the plumule from damage. When the cotyledons are free, the stem straightens. The cotyledons turn green and are the first leaves. They produce food by photosynthesis, and this helps the plumule to form the main shoot and larger leaves. This type of germination is called epigeal germination.

△ These sunflowers grew from seeds that all germinated at about the same time.

▽ The first two stages of sunflower germination are like those of peas. The radicle emerges (A) and root hairs start to grow (B). But then the growing shoot pulls the cotyledons out of the seed coat (C) and up into the air (D).

▷ Sunflower cotyledons function as true leaves when they emerge from the seed (E). Cotyledons are usually simpler than leaves that grow later.

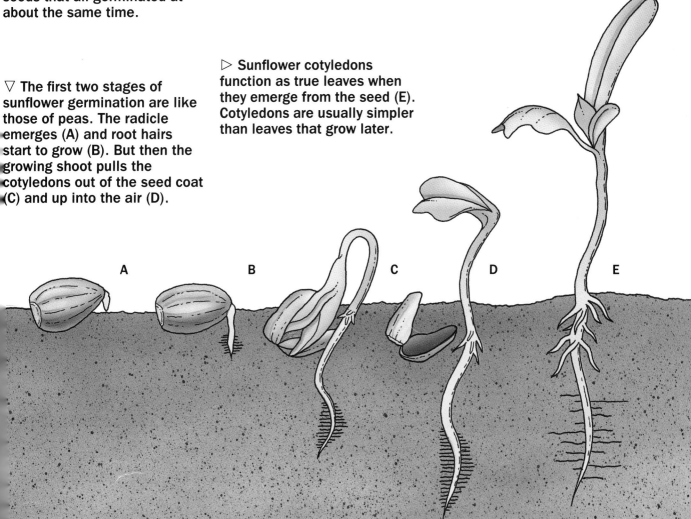

A   B   C   D   E

WHEAT

Wheat is one of the most important grain crops in the world. Its most common use is to produce flour for baking. Wheat grain provides a good combination of proteins and carbohydrates. It is easy to grow and the grains can be harvested cheaply using machines. Wheat grain can also be stored for a long time.

The wheat grain is a fruit with a single seed inside. Wheat is a monocotyledon. The food store fills the part of the seed outside the embryo. The cotyledon stays below ground during germination. It absorbs food from the store and passes it to the growing parts of the seedling. In wheat, the plumule grows straight up through the soil. The plumule is protected from damage by a tough cap called the coleoptile.

Soon, the first true leaves break through the coleoptile as the shoot grows. The cotyledon withers away as the food in the seed is used up. New roots do not grow from the radicle. Instead, they come singly from the base of the shoot.

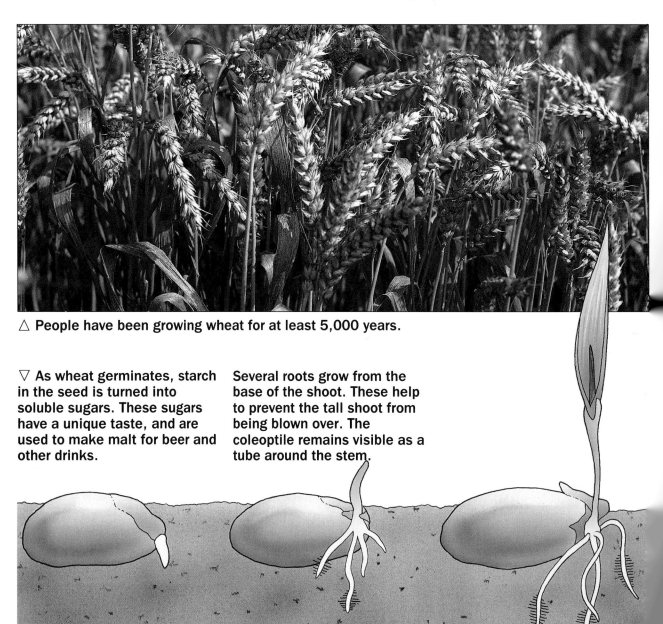

△ People have been growing wheat for at least 5,000 years.

▽ As wheat germinates, starch in the seed is turned into soluble sugars. These sugars have a unique taste, and are used to make malt for beer and other drinks.

Several roots grow from the base of the shoot. These help to prevent the tall shoot from being blown over. The coleoptile remains visible as a tube around the stem.

AFFECTING GROWTH

Seedlings behave in ways that increase their chances of finding sunlight, water and minerals.

This determines the response of shoots and roots to gravity. Shoots grow upward, away from gravity. Roots grow downward, toward gravity.

Sunlight affects the growth of shoots. Place cress seeds in good light and the seedlings will grow with stout but short stems. If they are placed in deep shade or darkness, the seedlings become tall and spindly. They grow tall in order to try to reach light.

Light has the opposite effect on radicles. It makes them grow long and spindly, and they produce no lateral roots. They are using all their energy trying to find the soil, where it is dark. The soil contains the mineral salts and water that the plant needs.

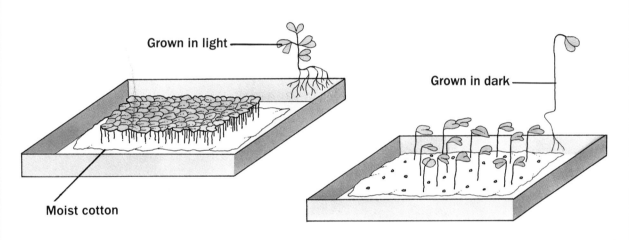

Grown in light

Moist cotton

Grown in dark

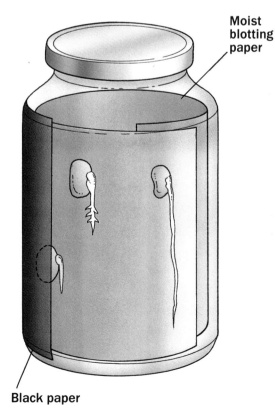

Moist blotting paper

In dark, strong root growth with lateral roots

In light, spindly pale growth

Black paper

◁ △ To test the effect of light on radicles, put beans in a jar, as in the picture. Cover half the jar with black paper and see what happens.

Learning Resources Center
University of Wyoming Libraries
Laramie, WY 82070

Roots have a number of different jobs. They anchor the plant, preventing the shoot from being toppled by the wind and the force of gravity. They absorb water from the soil, together with dissolved minerals. These substances are carried to the leafy shoots. Some plants have roots that store food for later use.

ROOT SYSTEMS

There is a good chance to examine roots when a tree is blown over in a storm. Large amounts of soil are often pulled up with the roots, although some roots break off in the ground. The tangle of roots on a plant is called the root system. The root system usually reaches out as far as the shoots or branches do. Sometimes, a thick main root can be seen. Smaller lateral roots grow out from the main root. This type of root system is called a tap root system. Tap roots often become swollen with stored food, as in the carrot, beet and parsnip. In other plants the roots are all of similar size. This is called a fibrous root system.

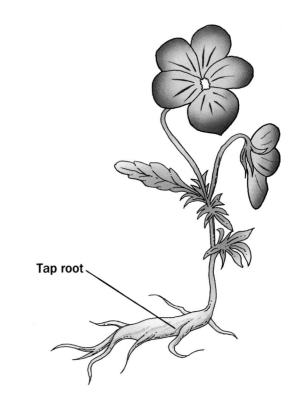

Tap root

STRUCTURE

Like all living organisms, plants are made up of tiny building blocks called cells. Different types of cells are grouped together to form tissues. Roots grow longer because cells in the tip of the root divide into two and enlarge.

Long thin cells called root hairs absorb water and minerals from the soil. The water and minerals then pass through the cortex and enter the xylem tissue. The xylem forms a star-shaped core which runs up and joins to xylem in the stem and leaves. Special tubular cells in the xylem carry the water up to the leaves. Food made in the leaves passes down to the growing root through the phloem tissue. The root cap protects the root tip as it pushes through the soil.

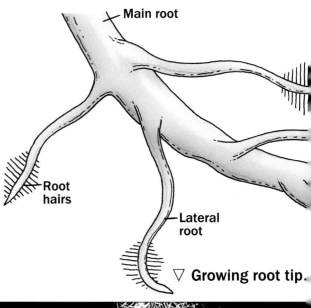

Main root

Root hairs

Lateral root

▽ Growing root tip.

◁ Tap root systems are found mainly in dicotyledons. Food stored in the root allows the plant to survive harsh periods, such as winter. Tap roots often grow to great depths in search of water.

▷ Most monocotyledons and many dicotyledons have fibrous root systems. The main roots grow from the base of the stem — in this case a bulb. These roots have smaller lateral roots than tap root systems do.

Fibrous root

RUCTURE

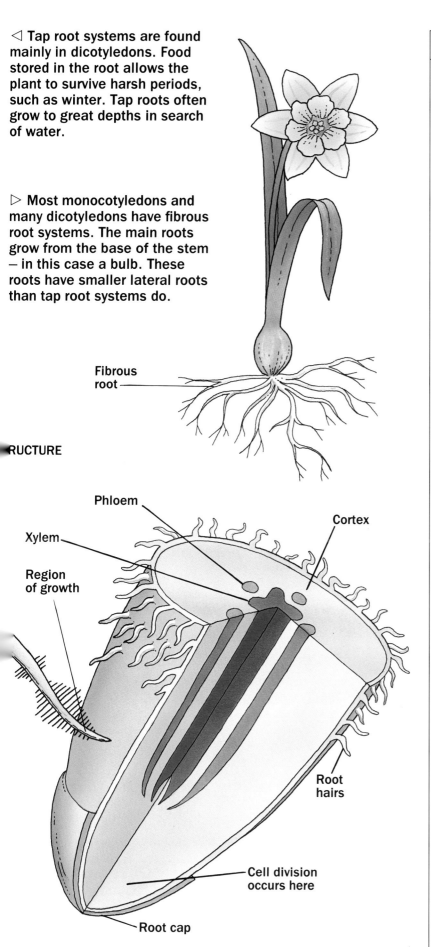

Phloem

Xylem

Region of growth

Cortex

Root hairs

Cell division occurs here

Root cap

EXPERIMENT

The importance of gravity in root growth is shown by this experiment. Cut a pad of blotting paper to fit tightly in the bottom of a jar. Fix three bean seeds to the pad using pins (do not stick them through the bean). Soak the paper and let the seeds germinate with the jar upright. Now set the jar on its side. The young roots bend and grow downward in response to gravity.

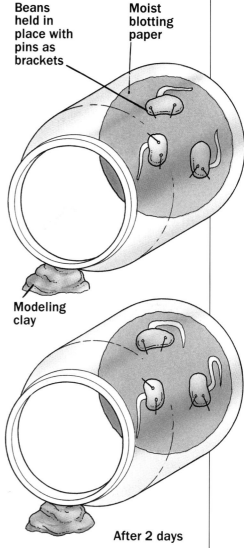

Beans held in place with pins as brackets

Moist blotting paper

Modeling clay

After 2 days

Stems form part of the shoot. Their main job is to support the leaves, buds and flowers. The way in which the leaves and flowers are exposed to sun and insects is very important. Plants often have green stems, which make food in the same way as leaves do. Stems also allow water and nutrients to be moved inside the plant.

CHARACTERISTICS

Each stem is made up of a number of similar units joined end to end. A stem unit consists of a straight piece of stem, known as an internode. Internodes join together at swollen areas called nodes. Leaves and buds are attached at the nodes. If a bud starts to grow, it can form a side branch or a flowering stem.

Usually there is an obvious main stem. If the main stem dies, a side stem can grow to take its place. The stems of plants that do not have leaves — like cacti — are the main place where food is formed. The "bulb" of the buttercup is a special food-storing stem. Such stems are called corms.

INSIDE STEMS

Two different types of growth occur in stems. Non-woody shoots grow by the division of cells in the stem tip. This occurs in all young stems. Later, woody tissues grow in dicotyledons.

The outer layer of non-woody stems is called the epidermis. It is covered by a waxy layer to prevent drying out. The xylem and phloem tissues are strands running up the stem. The phloem is on the outside and the xylem on the inside. Each strand runs to an individual leaf.

The height to which plants can grow depends on how strong the stem is. There is a substance called lignin that can form in xylem and some other tissues. It increases the strength of stems and makes them woody.

△ Flowers are held up by the strength of stems.

▽ Typical structure of a plant.

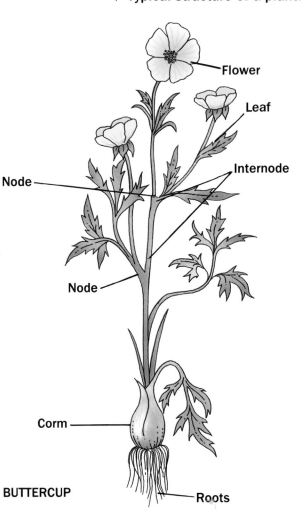

Flower

Leaf

Internode

Node

Node

Corm

BUTTERCUP

Roots

TOWARD THE LIGHT

Stems grow toward light. Place a potted plant on its side under bright light. After a few days the stem starts to bend upward. This is not caused by gravity. The stem also bends sideways if lit from the side. It bends because cells on the dark side grow faster than those on the light side.

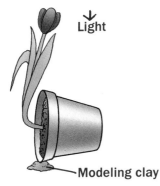
Light

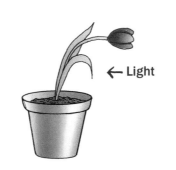
← Light

Modeling clay

DID YOU KNOW?

It is possible to tell the age of a tree by counting the number of rings in its trunk. These are known as growth rings. A new ring forms each year of the tree's life. The oldest living tree in the world is a bristlecone pine in California. It is more than 4,600 years old!

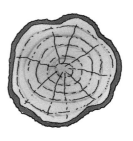

▽ This stem has formed cambium and is just about to start making woody growth.

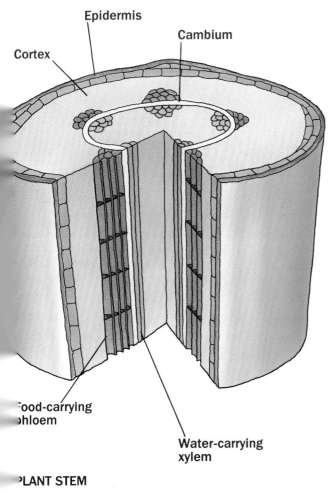

Epidermis

Cambium

Cortex

Food-carrying phloem

Water-carrying xylem

PLANT STEM

WOODY STEMS

Woody growth makes stems stronger and thicker, and allows strong boughs and branches to form. A ring of cells called the cambium runs up the stem. It passes between the xylem and phloem tissues, going through each of the strands. The cells in the cambium start to divide and form new xylem cells on the inside and new phloem on the outside. The xylem cells become soaked with lignin and form strong wood. Weaker cells form rays that radiate through the stem. Bark forms on the outside and makes the swelling stem waterproof.

▽ Wood forms in rings.

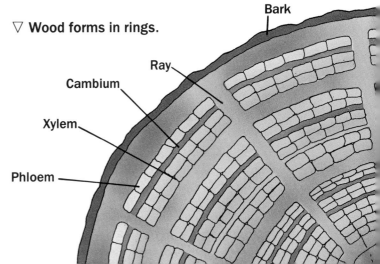
Bark

Ray

Cambium

Xylem

Phloem

Leaves come in a huge number of shapes and sizes, but they all have one function in common. They produce food for the plant by photosynthesis. The leaf changes the energy in sunlight, using a green pigment called chlorophyll. This energy is used to make sugar from carbon dioxide (CO_2) and water (H_2O).

STRUCTURE

Leaves are usually flat to trap as much sunlight as possible. They are also thin. If leaves were thick, some of the cells would not get enough light or CO_2 for photosynthesis, but would still need to use up food.

The leaf is kept firm by the midrib and veins. The midrib and veins have xylem to bring water from the stem. They also have phloem to take sugar that has been made in the leaf to the stem.

Photosynthesis happens inside the leaf cells. Palisade cells contain lots of chlorophyll and absorb most of the light. The spongy mesophyll layer has air spaces. CO_2 enters the leaf through holes on the underside called stomata.

△ Veins carry sugar and water around inside the leaf. In dicotyledons the veins usually form a branching network. The veins in monocotyledons are arranged in parallel lines.

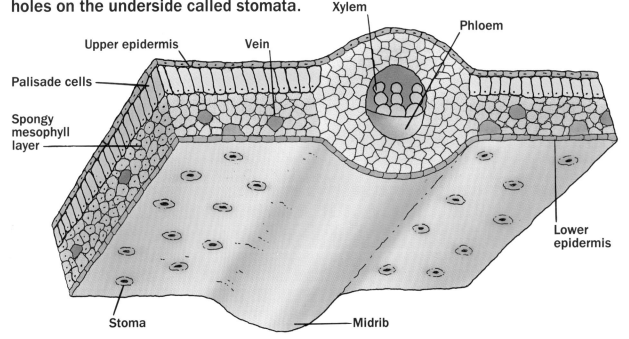

Xylem

Phloem

Upper epidermis

Vein

Palisade cells

Spongy mesophyll layer

Lower epidermis

Stoma

Midrib

△ The epidermis is covered in a waxy layer called the cuticle. This helps to prevent the leaf from losing water and wilting. But the cuticle also keeps CO_2 out, so there are stomata to let CO_2 enter the leaf. They are usually on the shaded side to keep water loss small.

BREATHING

Stomata are special pores that control the movement of gases in and out of leaves. Each stoma can be opened or closed. The stomata open during the day to let CO_2 into the leaf for photosynthesis. In bright sunshine, lots of water evaporates from the mesophyll cells and passes out through the stomata. If the soil is dry, the plant could wilt and die. To prevent this, the stomata close in very dry weather. They also close at night.

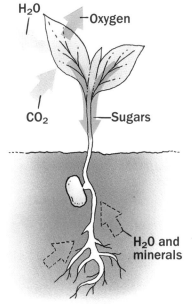

H_2O Oxygen CO_2 Sugars H_2O and minerals

△ In photosynthesis, CO_2 and H_2O are combined to form sugars using energy from sunlight. Oxygen is given out as a waste product. There was no oxygen in the atmosphere before plants appeared on Earth and produced it.

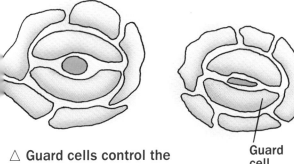
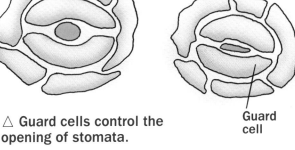

△ Guard cells control the opening of stomata.

Guard cell

LEAF ARRANGEMENTS

Leaves usually fit around the stem in a way that catches the most sunlight. They position themselves so that one leaf is in the shade of others as little as possible. Stand under a beech tree and notice how the leaves seem to fit together and blot out the sky.

▽ Three different arrangements of leaves.

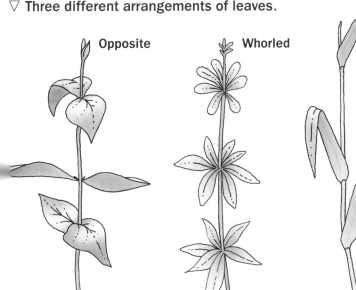

Opposite   Whorled   Alternate

DID YOU KNOW?

The enormous leaves of the giant water lily from the Amazon can support the weight of a child. The raised rim of each leaf acts like the sides of a boat. Thick veins keep the leaf from folding up as it floats on the water.

Most countries have both good and poor seasons for plant growth. Plants often grow when conditions are good, but form buds to pass through the poor season. Buds are miniature shoots with a stem and tightly packed leaves or flowers. They can rapidly expand into leafy shoots when good conditions return.

STRUCTURE

Deciduous plants form buds and lose their leaves as the winter approaches. Good examples are the broadleaf trees like oak, beech and horse chestnut. Many other plants form winter buds even though they are not fully deciduous. The buds are a safeguard against very severe frosts, which may kill all the green shoots.

Buds are formed during the summer. This happens when the tree senses that the days are becoming shorter. Usually a large bud forms at the end of each shoot or twig. Smaller buds form in the leaf axils – the angles between each leaf and the stem. Each bud is surrounded by small, tough leaves called bud scales.

During the winter the buds stay dormant. This dormancy is broken by a signal that spring has arrived. In trees, the signal is often a rise in temperature after a period of cold.

△ Buds contain next year's shoots and flowers.

▽ The large winter buds of horse chestnut are often called "sticky buds." The horse chestnut is one of the earliest trees to come into leaf in the spring. The buds start to swell as the stem inside lengthens (A). As the bud scales bend back, fluffy leaves can be seen inside (B). These are folded up in the bud, but now start to expand (C). The stem starts to grow from the bud, pushing the leaves upward (D).

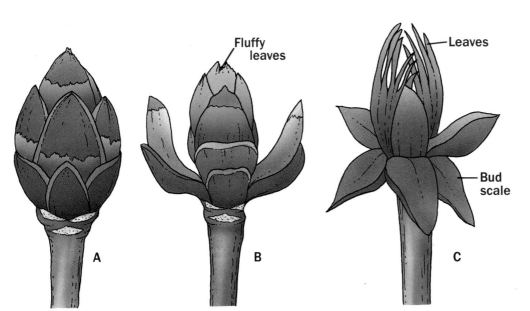

Fluffy leaves

Leaves

Stem

Bud scale

A   B   C

LEAF FALL

All trees shed their leaves. Deciduous trees lose all their leaves at once in the autumn. Evergreens drop leaves in ones and twos all through the year. A few deciduous trees lose their leaves in very hot conditions. Getting rid of the leaves helps to stop the tree from drying up when the soil is frozen or very dry.

Deciduous trees prepare for leaf fall in late summer. They sense the shortening days or lower temperatures. Useful substances are withdrawn from the leaves. This is what causes them to change from green to red or yellow. A layer of cork forms at the bottom of the leaf stalk. The leaf falls off when the weak cells in the cork layer break.

▽ Scars left by leaves do not form rings.

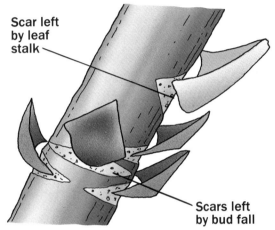

Scar left by leaf stalk

Scars left by bud fall

△ Deciduous forests change color in autumn.

▽ The leaves take on their final shape (E). As the bud scales drop they leave a ring of scars around the twig (F).

DID YOU KNOW?

Dragon trees, like this one on Tenerife, are some of the few monocotyledons to form wood. Some species of dragon tree produce a red resin which is known as "dragon's blood."

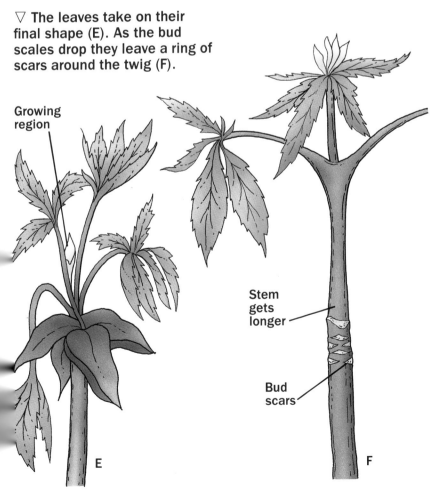

Growing region

Stem gets longer

Bud scars

E

F

Flowers are the special parts of plants that make seeds for reproduction. They also carry the structures that are necessary for pollination. Reproduction that involves pollination and seeds is one form of sexual reproduction. Plants and their flowers are often both male and female at the same time.

STRUCTURE

The parts of a flower are arranged in rings (known as whorls) around the stem or stalk. Sepals protect the flower in the bud. They are usually green. The petals are usually larger and often colored.

The male parts of a flower are called the stamens. Stamens are made up of anthers on top of stalks called filaments. Pollen forms inside the anthers. The female parts are called the carpels. The top of the carpel (the stigma) traps pollen. Below this is the style, and inside is an ovule. The ovule will later form the seed. All the parts of a flower join to a receptacle, which is an enlarged part of the stem.

△ Brightly colored flowers attract insects. The insects feed on sugar produced by the nectaries and on pollen.

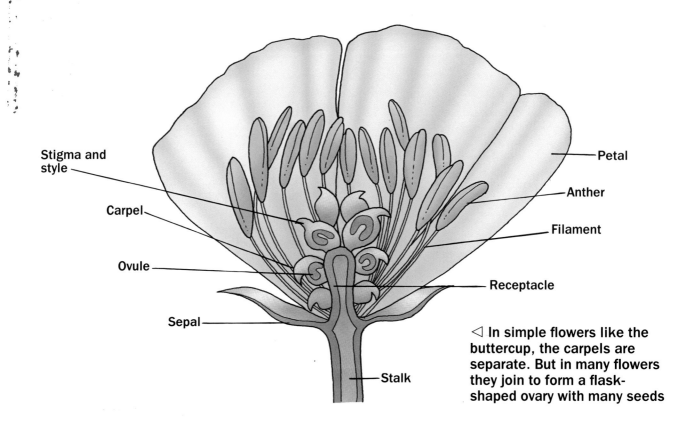

Stigma and style

Carpel

Ovule

Sepal

Petal

Anther

Filament

Receptacle

Stalk

◁ In simple flowers like the buttercup, the carpels are separate. But in many flowers they join to form a flask-shaped ovary with many seeds

POLLINATION

Pollination is the name given to the transfer of pollen from anthers to stigmas. This transfer is necessary for seeds to form. Movement of the pollen may be brought about by insects or sometimes by other animals. Pollen is also often carried in the wind and sometimes by moving water. Many flowers are specially structured to undergo pollination by only one of these methods.

Insect-pollinated flowers are usually easy to see and brightly colored. The male and female parts are often hidden inside. Wind-pollinated flowers have small green petals and no nectaries or scent. The anthers hang out to shed pollen. The stigmas are feathery to catch pollen that is blowing past.

Pollination between flowers on separate plants is known as cross-pollination. It allows characteristics of the parents to be mixed in new ways. This lets the species adapt if living conditions change. Pollination between flowers on the same plant, or even within the same flower, is known as self-pollination. It does not allow mixing of characteristics.

△ Catkins shed large amounts of pollen into the air.

Cross-pollination

Self-pollination

△▷ In cross-pollination, the pollen is carried from an anther on one plant to a stigma on another plant. Self-pollination is transfer of pollen between an anther and a stigma on the same plant.

Self-pollination

LEARNING RESOURCES CENTER
UNIVERSITY OF WYOMING
LARAMIE, WY 82071

ANIMAL POLLINATION

Plants such as buttercups have simple flowers that are open and regular in shape. They can be pollinated by almost any small creature that crawls onto them. But because of their simple shape, self-pollination often occurs.

Many flowers have a design that increases the chances of cross-pollination by insects. In one sort of design, the petals are joined together to form a tube. The nectaries are at the bottom of the tube. Insects have to crawl into the tube to feed from the nectaries. They are then more likely to brush against the anthers and stigmas.

The petals of insect-pollinated flowers are often different sizes. Special petals provide a place for insects to land. Colored lines — called honey guides — help insects to find the flower tube. Only insects of the right size and shape can enter these flowers and cause pollination. This helps to make pollination more likely, because pollen will not be wasted on insects that can go to lots of different species of flower.

Many flowers are pollinated by bees and butterflies. Pollen easily sticks to their hairy bodies. These insects have long tongues to reach the nectar.

△ Hummingbirds need lots of sugary nectar. They visit and pollinate large, brightly colored flowers.

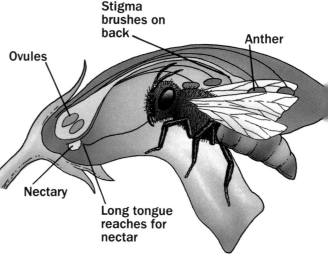

Ovules
Stigma brushes on back
Anther
Nectary
Long tongue reaches for nectar

△ The white deadnettle is pollinated by bees with long tongues. As the bee pushes into the flower the stigma and anthers brush on its back.

◁ The lower petals of lupin and gorse flowers are pushed down by the weight of a bee when it lands. The stigma and anthers brush the bee's underside.

Pollen brushed on abdomen and legs

Ovules

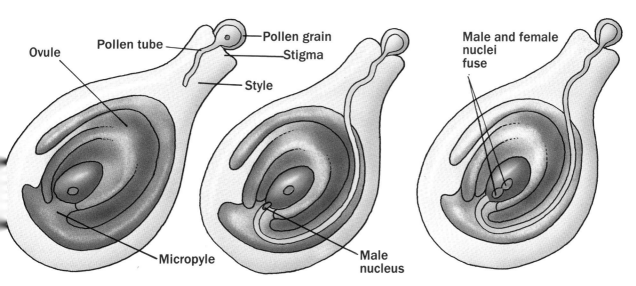

Ovule — Pollen tube — Pollen grain — Stigma — Style — Micropyle — Male and female nuclei fuse — Male nucleus

△ When a pollen grain lands on a stigma, a pollen tube starts to grow.

△ A pollen tube grows down through the style, through the micropyle, and into the ovule.

△ The male nucleus passes down the pollen tube and fuses with the nucleus in the ovule.

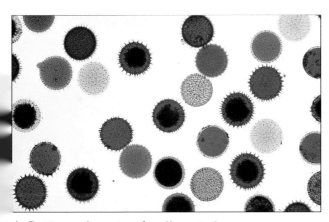

△ Patterned coats of pollen grains

DID YOU KNOW?

Honey possums feed entirely on pollen and nectar using a brush-tipped tongue. They dart from flower to flower. Like insects, they help to pollinate the flowers.

▽ A honey possum in Australia

FERTILIZATION

Seeds are formed by sexual reproduction. In sexual reproduction, special cells called gametes are produced by male and female plants or animals. These cells fuse (join together) in a process called fertilization. In flowers, this happens after pollination. The male gamete is the pollen grain and the female gamete is an egg cell inside the ovule.

During pollination, grains of pollen become stuck to the stigma. If the pollen and stigma are of the same species, the pollen grain sends out a pollen tube. The pollen tube grows down through the style into the swollen part of the carpel, which contains the ovule. Only one tube reaches the ovule, and the rest die. The successful pollen tube enters the ovule through the micropyle.

When fertilization happens, the end of the pollen tube breaks. A tiny particle called a nucleus moves from the tube into the ovule. This fuses with the female nucleus of the egg cell.

The fertilized ovule now grows into a seed inside the ovary. If the flower contains several ovules inside an ovary, a separate pollen grain fertilizes the egg cell in each of the ovules.

FRUIT FORMATION

The final event in the life cycle of a flowering plant is the formation of seeds and fruits.

After fertilization, the petals, sepals, stamens, styles and stigmas start to shrivel up. The fertilized egg cell divides many times to form the tissues of the embryo. Other cells in the ovule divide to form a food store known as endosperm. The outer layers of the ovule form the testa. The micropyle remains as a hole in the coat of the ripe seed. It sometimes lets water enter the seed at germination.

Fruits develop from the ovary. The number of seeds in the fruit depends on the number of carpels that joined to form the ovary. Fruits called multiple fruits are formed from several ovaries.

△ Fruits form if the ovule is fertilized.

▽ Sometimes parts of the flower besides the ovary help to form the fruit. The apple flower has a receptacle that encloses the ovary. The outer flesh of the apple is formed from the receptacle. The true fruit wall can be seen as a line.

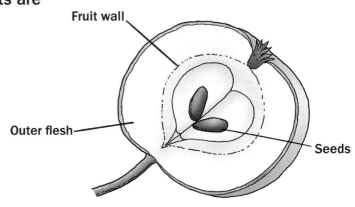

RIPE FRUIT

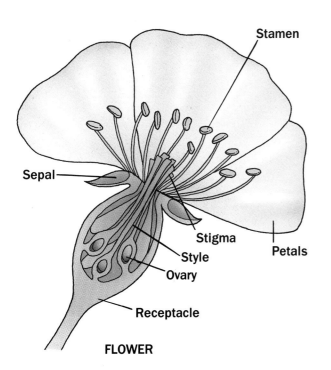

FLOWER

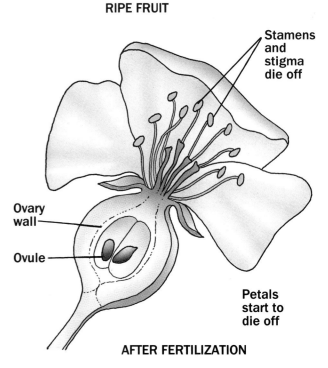

AFTER FERTILIZATION

DIFFERENT FRUITS

See how many different kinds of fruits you can find. Remember that vegetables like peas in their pods are actually fruits.

Examine each fruit carefully and try and understand how it has formed. Get an adult to help cut the fruit open so that you can see the number and arrangement of the seeds. Can you see if there is more than one ovary? Is the fruit dehiscent or is it indehiscent?

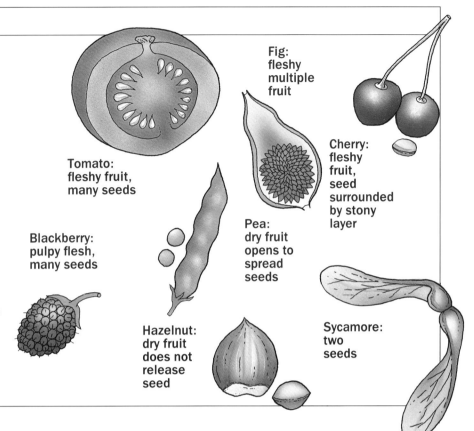

Tomato: fleshy fruit, many seeds

Fig: fleshy multiple fruit

Cherry: fleshy fruit, seed surrounded by stony layer

Blackberry: pulpy flesh, many seeds

Pea: dry fruit opens to spread seeds

Hazelnut: dry fruit does not release seed

Sycamore: two seeds

▽ The stigmas in rose-bay willow herb are raised above the anthers. This lessens the chance of self-pollination occurring. The ovary is formed from fused carpels. Willow herb fruits are dehiscent. They split open when they are ripe. The seeds have strands that act like parachutes for wind dispersal.

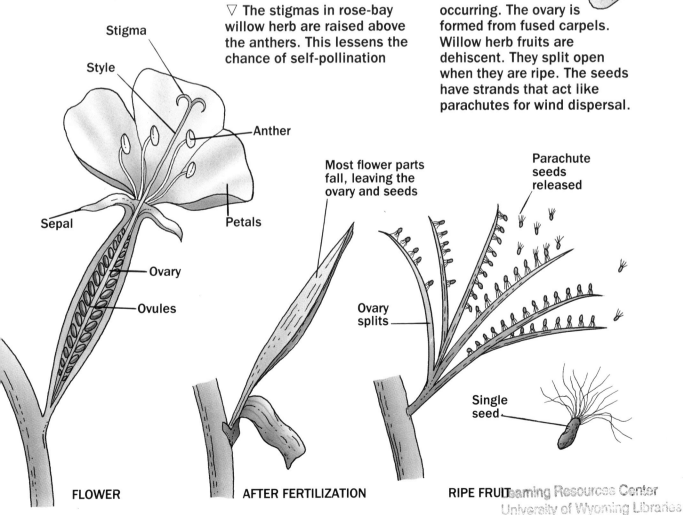

Stigma

Style

Anther

Sepal

Petals

Ovary

Ovules

Most flower parts fall, leaving the ovary and seeds

Parachute seeds released

Ovary splits

Single seed

FLOWER

AFTER FERTILIZATION

RIPE FRUIT

Learning Resources Center
University of Wyoming Libraries
Laramie, WY 82070

Seeds are usually the only method of reproduction in annual plants – ones that complete their life cycle in a year and die. Many perennial species – those that live for several years – also reproduce vegetatively. Offshoots grow from the parent plant, then become separate and start to live on their own.

△ Onions are typical bulbs.

BULBS AND CORMS

Perennial plants often store food made during good weather for later use. The food is stored in the parts, or organs, that can produce new plants. Producing new plants without using seeds is known as vegetative propagation.

A corm is simply a short piece of stem that is swollen with food. It survives the winter, or (in some species) hot, dry periods, underground. Buds are formed on the corm before the leaves die down. Later, the main bud forms new leaves using the food in the corm. These leaves produce a new corm on top of the old one. Other buds may also grow into shoots that form corms. So one corm can produce several new corms. Each new corm grows special roots called contractile roots. When fully grown, these roots shrink and pull the corm deeper into the soil.

Bulbs are mostly made of small fleshy leaves that store food. These leaves are called bulb scales. At the bottom of the bulb there is a piece of stem. Roots grow down from this. Each year the main bud grows to form new leaves and flowers. Food produced by the leaves helps to make new scales inside the bulb as the outer ones die. New bulbs can form if other buds, called lateral buds, grow.

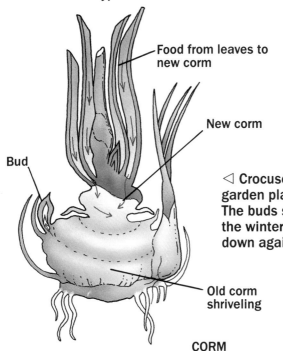

Food from leaves to new corm

New corm

Bud

Old corm shriveling

CORM

◁ Crocuses are common garden plants that have corms. The buds start to grow early in the winter and the leaves die down again by early summer.

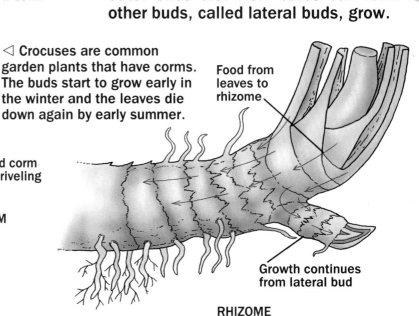

Food from leaves to rhizome

Growth continues from lateral bud

RHIZOME

▷ Many iris species have rhizomes, although some have bulbs. The tip of the iris rhizome turns up to form the leaves and flowering shoot.

▽ Strawberries propagate by runners growing from the stem.

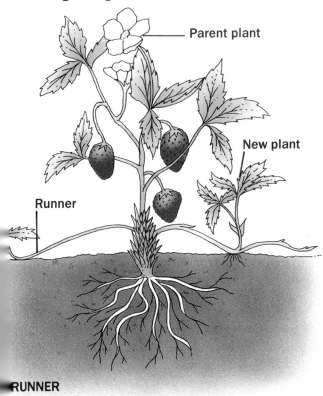

Parent plant

New plant

Runner

RUNNER

RUNNERS, RHIZOMES AND TUBERS

Runners, rhizomes and tubers are also organs for vegetative propagation.

Runners are horizontal stems that grow from buds on an adult plant. New plants develop on the runner from buds at the nodes. Roots grow down into the soil to anchor the new plant.

Rhizomes are similar to runners, but they grow underground. In irises, food is stored in the rhizome. Leaves and flowers form when the end of the rhizome grows upward. New rhizomes start to grow from lateral buds.

Potatoes are examples of special rhizomes called tubers. Ordinary rhizomes grow out from the potato plant. The ends swell and store food. The "eyes" of potatoes are compressed stems with buds. These turn into next year's plants.

▽ Bulbs are produced by spring flowering plants like snowdrops, daffodils and bluebells.

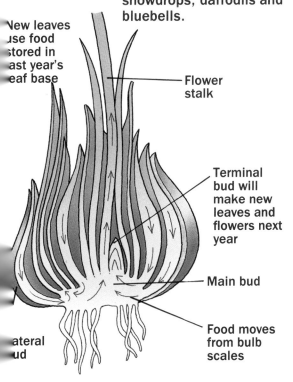

New leaves use food stored in last year's leaf base

Flower stalk

Terminal bud will make new leaves and flowers next year

Main bud

Lateral bud

Food moves from bulb scales

Roots

BULB

POTATO PROJECT

It is easy to grow potatoes. Fill a large pot with earth. Plant a single tuber four inches deep. Remember to water the pot sometimes. Examine the new tubers when the plant is flowering.

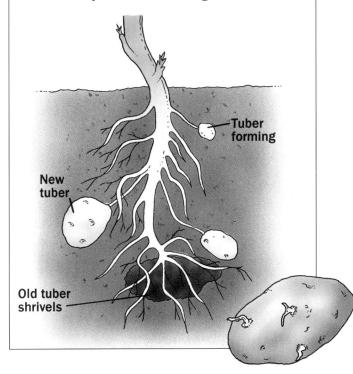

Tuber forming

New tuber

Old tuber shrivels

Putting living species into groups of similar kinds is called classification. This book talks about the group of plants that is most important to people, the flowering plants or angiosperms.

The chart below includes all the major groups of plants. This arrangement is called a natural classification. It arranges plants and their relatives with simple types at one end and complex kinds at the other. Simple kinds, like some algae, were among the first living organisms to appear on Earth (about three billion years ago). The angiosperms did not appear until near the end of the age of dinosaurs (about 65 million years ago).

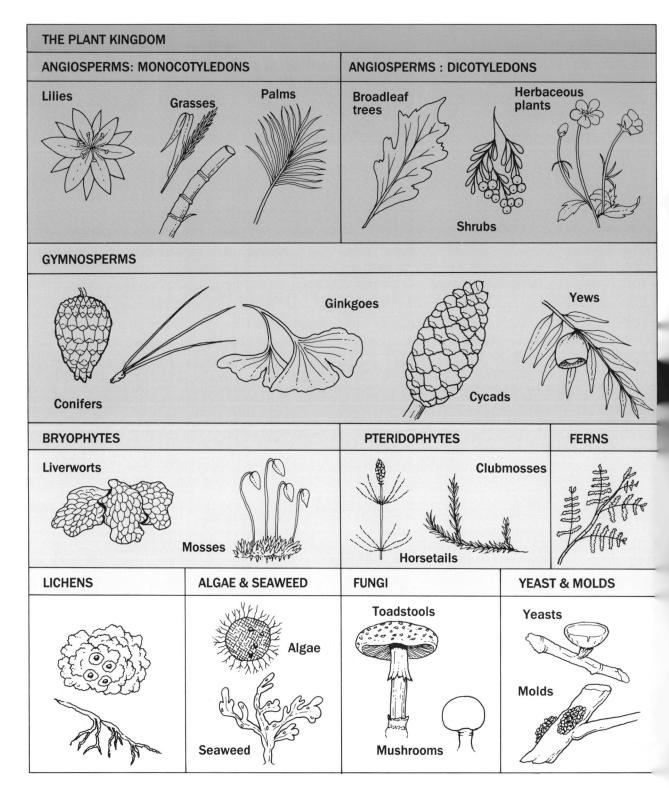

THE PLANT KINGDOM

ANGIOSPERMS: MONOCOTYLEDONS

Lilies Grasses Palms

ANGIOSPERMS : DICOTYLEDONS

Broadleaf trees Herbaceous plants

Shrubs

GYMNOSPERMS

Ginkgoes Yews

Conifers Cycads

BRYOPHYTES

Liverworts

Mosses

PTERIDOPHYTES

Clubmosses

Horsetails

FERNS

LICHENS

ALGAE & SEAWEED

Algae

Seaweed

FUNGI

Toadstools

Mushrooms

YEAST & MOLDS

Yeasts

Molds

Anther
One of the male parts of a flower. It produces pollen.

Carpel
The female parts of a flower.

Chlorophyll
A green pigment that traps the energy of sunlight for use in photosynthesis.

Cotyledon
A leaf of the embryo in a seed.

Fertilization
In plants, the fusion of a male pollen nucleus with a female nucleus inside the ovule.

Fruit
Tissue that surrounds a seed and is formed from the ovary. Indehiscent fruits are dispersed with the seed. Dehiscent fruits split open to release the seed for dispersal.

Germination
The growth of a seed into a seedling.

Nectary
A swelling, usually at the base of a flower. It produces a sugary solution called nectar which is attractive to insects.

Organ
Any part of a plant (or animal) that has a particular function, such as a root.

Ovary
A female part of a flower. It is composed of one or more joined carpels, each containing one ovule.

Phloem
The tissue in which sugars move from leaves to other parts of a plant.

Photosynthesis
The process in which green plants use energy from sunlight to convert carbon dioxide and water into sugars.

Plumule
The growing tip of the young shoot in a seed embryo.

Pollination
The transfer of pollen grains from an anther to a stigma.

Radicle
The young root of a seed embryo.

Rhizome
An underground organ of vegetative propagation.

Seed
The result of fertilization of an ovule. It consists of a plant embryo and its food store enclosed by a protective coat.

Stomata
The breathing holes in a leaf. Each is called a stoma and consists of a pore and two guard cells which can close it.

Tissue
Any living material that is made up of cells, for example, root tissue.

Vegetative propagation
Reproduction of a plant not involving seeds, for example, by a corm.

Wood
Xylem tissue that has a large amount of lignin. It is formed by division of cells in the cambium.

Xylem
The tissue that conducts water and dissolved minerals from the roots to other parts of a plant.

Photographic Credits:
Cover and pages 5, 7 top and bottom,
10-11, 24 and 25 top: Robert Harding
Picture Library; pages 6, 8, 16 and 28:
F. Killerby; pages 12, 20, 21 top, 22 and
26: Spectrum Photo Library; page 14:
Science Photo Library; pages 19 bottom
and 23: Eye Ubiquitous; page 21 bottom:
J. Allan Cash Photo Library; page 25
bottom: Bruce Coleman Photo Library.

PRINTED IN BELGIUM BY
proost
INTERNATIONAL BOOK PRODUCTION